# CODE NAME KC:

## *A True Account of One Osprey*

by Linda Zeltzer

Photography by
Julian K. Robinson

Dedicated

to my husband, Bob, for his

unwavering support in all things

## ACKNOWLEDGMENTS

To my grown-up kids, Karen, Steven, and Deb; to my sister, Steffie; and to my niece, Jocelyn — thank you for the enthusiasm you have always shown for all my stories. To grandchildren, Joshua, Isabel, and Jenna (my young readers) and to Lily and Oliver (my future readers), welcome to the world of raptors. I am indebted to the always gracious Julian Robinson for the use of his stunning shots of KC and other Vineyard ospreys; to Gus Ben David, for sitting so willingly as I read the manuscript aloud in its entirety; to Pamela Greenwood, from whom I learned much about writing for children; to Jackie Mendez-Diez, for her keen editorial insights; and to Janet Holladay, of Tisbury Printer, for her expert guidance in book design.

For ordering information, contact
Cranberry Hill Press
P.O. Box 419
Chilmark, MA 02535

# CONTENTS

KC had to go.

He left in September as he had the year before, and the years before that. His journey would be filled with danger. He could die trying to reach his winter destination or die attempting to return in the spring.

This is the account of one amazing osprey that summered at Felix Neck Wild Life Sanctuary on Martha's Vineyard, an island off the coast of Massachusetts.

KC was lucky for several reasons. First, nature endowed him with superior strength and stamina. Second, he summered on Martha's Vineyard, a beautiful island that attracts people from all over the world. This good fortune didn't impress him though. He would do whatever he did no matter where he lived because he was driven by instinct. But third, and probably the greatest piece of luck, the Vineyard is also the home of Gus Ben David.

KC's story begins with Gus. Gus was the director of the Massachusetts Audubon Society's Felix Neck Wild Life Sanctuary. Long ago, he coordinated the efforts of many people to save the osprey population in the area from extinction.

Learning about the past often helps us to understand the present and to change the future, as Gus did. So let's leave KC perched on his nest, and Gus as he surveys an area for a new nesting platform, and move back in time.

# A WARNING

When your grandparents were young, large numbers of osprey lived in many parts of this country. By the time your mom and dad were your age, the osprey population was nearly wiped out.

What happened during this period to endanger the ospreys and cause their babies to die before they were even born? Probably you haven't heard of DDT. And that's a good thing. DDT is a pesticide that was developed to kill insects. Insects destroy food crops. Insects carry disease. Insects annoy and bite people. The pesticide worked well. But it was also damaging the environment, and no one knew it.

When DDT was sprayed, it seeped into the water and into tiny plant and animal organisms called plankton. Plankton float in bodies of water. Small fish eat plankton.

DDT from the plankton stayed in their body tissue. Big fish eat small fish. The chemical accumulated in their bodies. Ospreys eat big fish. DDT built up in their system too.

When this happened, the pesticide contaminated them and affected their ability to have babies. DDT prevents the female from producing enough calcium for her eggshells. Without enough calcium, eggshells are too thin. When the mother sits on her eggs, they crack and break. Over time, if new chicks don't hatch, the population is wiped out.

Ospreys are raptors. A raptor is a bird of prey. Other raptors, like eagles, falcons, and owls eat rodents. These birds were dying too because the rodents absorbed the pesticides sprayed on weeds and crops.

This was a warning sign. Pesticides were poisoning the food chain. DDT was banned when its harmful effects became known.

Slowly, the raptor population began to increase again.

# A PLAN

Martha's Vineyard is a perfect habitat for ospreys because, as an island, it's surrounded by water that has a plentiful supply of food. KC must live near water because, like all ospreys, he eats only fish.

As a species of hawk, ospreys also go by the name "fish hawk" because of their exclusive fish diet. Deep-water fishing is difficult for these birds, though, so KC relies on shallow coastal ponds, shorelines, and beach areas for his meals.

And, like all ospreys, KC is not fussy where he builds his nest as long as he can build it high off the ground away from climbing predators, with open sky above the nest for easy landing, and an abundant food supply nearby. If there were no tall trees, KC would be content on top of a utility pole or on an artificial platform made especially for ospreys by people.

However, KC would never have made Felix Neck his home if there had not been ospreys living there before him. Just as you would not want to live in a place where there are no other human beings, the same is true of ospreys. They prefer to be with their own kind.

This characteristic posed a challenge more than thirty years ago. In the 1970s, before KC was even born, there were only two pairs of osprey left on the Island. Was there a way to attract more of these endangered birds so that they would find mates, build nests, and reproduce?

Gus Ben David devised a plan. He and a group of volunteers erected nesting poles with platforms. An Island electric company provided the poles. Over time, birds took up residence on the poles, establishing their territory for the purpose of breeding. Once a male and female are attracted to each other and build a nest, they return to the same site each year.

Slowly, the osprey colony grew. Now there are 114 nest poles scattered over the Island and approximately 75 breeding pairs each year.

# KC COMES TO
# FELIX NECK

KC showed up at Felix Neck one spring, took a mate, and settled in. As the Sanctuary's resident male, he held celebrity status for over twelve summers. Come follow the life of this splendid raptor and learn why.

KC is an enormous bird, reaching nearly two feet tall with a wingspan of five feet. Like other males, he has a brownish-black body, a white belly, and a white head with a black eye stripe. Females have similar plumage but usually have dark spotted feathers near their throat area.

Such large birds need big nests. Although some nests are bigger than others, imagine a nest up to six feet wide and weighing hundreds of pounds! Room enough for you and a friend to stretch out and take a nap—that is, if the "home owners" are away.

And what a project for KC and his mate! The couple can make over one hundred trips a day to haul up the sticks, branches, vines, driftwood, clumps of seaweed, and other debris ospreys utilize to build their home, which, when completed, will be sturdy enough for several years of occupancy.

# FAMILY LIFE

It's May, a bright, warm day in early morning. Island life quickens with activity and the promise of renewal. By now, the ospreys that successfully mated have active nests with, typically, two to three eggs.

However, successful breeding may vary from year to year. Some couples produce no young, but this is not unusual. They may be newly acquainted and need an adjustment period before becoming parents. They will try again the following

year. Sometimes a pair lays eggs but fails to raise chicks, or bad weather can be responsible for empty nests.

KC and his mate have an active nest. She is incubating eggs that will hatch in five to six weeks. When the chicks emerge, they will weigh only a few ounces—tiny considering mom and dad's size. Meanwhile, mom's job is to stay put for several months—a test of patience for any mother.

Dad's job is to hunt for two. Soaring to a height that can reach 100 feet above the ocean, KC is a marvel of nature. Sharp eyesight, estimated to be close to eight times keener than human eyesight, enables him to see several feet beneath the surface of the water, even from great heights.

KC's mate communicates her hunger by producing incessant begging calls for food. If ignored, her clamor intensifies causing quite a racket. "K-yewk, k-yewk!"

This time KC responds. Off he goes out over the ocean. He hovers and spots his prey. With the speed of an arrow shot from a bow, he reaches the water in seconds where, an instant before plunging, he reverses his headfirst direction, throws back his wings and enters feet-first.

He strikes! The thrashing, slippery fish can't escape the deadly grip of his feet, equipped with needle-like spikes called spicules, and talons, sharp as knives. Moments later, KC is flying back to the nest, carrying a meal for himself and his hungry mate.

Life continues like this for several weeks. Mom sits on the nest, and dad hunts, lugging back struggling prey like flounder, or if the couple is lucky, herring,

their favorite. Then one day in June, three little heads are visible in the nest.

Raising the babies is full-time work. Now KC must feed himself, his mate, and his chicks. He spends many hours flying, diving, and bringing fish back to the nest. This daily physical exertion places a

heavy burden on KC's energy level, so he consumes the largest portion of what he catches for calories and continued stamina.

Mom tears pieces from her share of the fish and feeds them to the chicks. She reduces her own portion, to provide sufficient food for their rapid growth, which will, in a month's time, reach 80% of their adult body weight.

Throughout the summer, the nest is a whirl of activity. The devoted parents struggle to feed their ever- hungry chicks, protect them from predators, and teach them, through imitation, how to lift and spread their wings.

During their "schooling," they gain muscles and strength by standing in the nest and beating their wings. This gymnastic display prepares them for flight and independence. Flying lessons follow. Urging their offspring to leave the nest takes noisy coaxing.

Soon they are ready to be fledged. This stage in their development means that they can leave the nest on their own to fly and explore, further developing strong wings and the confidence they will need to be self sufficient, but they are not yet independent. They still rely on their parents to bring them food.

During the last days before full independence, their parents do not feed them. This forces the young birds to attempt to hunt on their own, a skill they must develop quickly if they are to survive, because mom and dad's job is over. In a few days, they will leave their young behind and fly to wintering grounds thousands of miles away.

# A DANGEROUS
# JOURNEY

In late summer and early fall, ospreys from most parts of the United States leave their summer breeding grounds and migrate to Central or South America. The impulse to migrate is instinctive. This means that leaving one place to go to another place is not a thinking action.

Osprey behavior is controlled by urges they are born with—like seeking a mate or building a nest. They do what nature intends them to do. What makes these birds leave about the same time every year? How do they know when to go? It may be shorter day light hours that send the message. Another factor could be a dwindling food supply, since shallow-swimming fish, the osprey's staple, avoid the surface of colder water.

And how do they find their way? How do they know the direction to take and the routes to follow from one continent to another? Scientists think that the height of the sun above the horizon guides them. Ospreys that have migrated before may even recognize landmarks such as mountains and ocean coastlines.

Fall migration is underway. Without fanfare or backward glance, by mid-morning KC is gone. A few days later, his mate follows. Traveling alone, like all their species, they have joined the annual osprey

exodus south. Each will need strength, endurance, and luck to survive this long and dangerous journey.

# BEATING THE ODDS

Two weeks have passed at Felix Neck. It is enough time for KC's youngsters to grow stronger flight muscles and become competent hunters. But nothing in their upbringing has prepared them for what lies ahead.

Instinct tells them it's time. The young birds spread their wings. Flap! Flap! Up, up they lift, high above their snug-nesting universe to a world beyond that is wild and strange and full of peril. There are no maps, no geography lessons, no familiar landmarks, no grown-ups to lead the way. Remarkably, nature's built-in compass will help them to navigate their first flight to South America, over two thousand miles away.

Like their parents, they travel alone. The hazards are great for both young and older birds. Death is common. They may die in severe storms or hurricanes. Some are killed in accidents. Others die from injuries. Or hunters sometimes shoot them. Seeking rest and shelter, ospreys often land on ships—only to be killed by someone on board.

Crossing the Caribbean Sea is especially dangerous because of its five hundred miles of open water. Flying non-stop with nowhere to rest, and unable to hunt in deep water, even the most powerful ospreys may succumb to exhaustion and

starvation. If KC's offspring survive the grueling trip, they will spend the next two years—the time it takes to reach breeding age—in Venezuela. At the end of two years, they will leave and travel all the way back to Martha's Vineyard, the place of their birth.

Amazingly, they will closely duplicate their first migration route, visiting the same places for rest and food. If they beat the odds and complete the risky migration, each will take a mate and set up housekeeping, although they don't successfully reproduce until the age of three or four.

There's no telling if KC and his mate safely completed their migration south. If they did, they will join other ospreys who generally congregate in flocks and spend their time perching together, resting and fishing. A winter sojourn lasts from about November through February—perhaps a period of relief for some over-worked parents.

Then the urge to reproduce triggers the cycle again. Spring migration brings the return of the ospreys to their nesting sites in the north. Their flight back poses the same challenges. Those who make it, ensure the future of their species.

# BACKPACKS AND SATELLITES

KC's aerial descent was sudden and unannounced. Into his old nest he dropped! Gus felt relief at seeing him.

Every spring it was the same—not knowing if he'd make it. KC's mate was not as fortunate. Somewhere, she perished. But KC lost no time in finding another companion.

Ospreys are loyal to the nest they build, not to each other. Nature compels them to pass their genes on to the next genera-

tion, so any mate will do. For the moment, KC is engaged in housekeeping with his new partner, unaware that soon he would play a leading role in a fascinating study called "Highway to the Tropics."

The Highway to the Tropics project was conducted by the Raptor Center at the University of Minnesota College of Veterinary Medicine. The Center specializes in taking care of birds of prey. Scientists developed a program to track the migratory routes of ospreys from their breeding grounds to their wintering locations. This extraordinary program involved solar-powered radio transmitters and satellites in space.

A number of ospreys from different regions of the country were equipped with radio transmitters harnessed to them like little backpacks. The transmitters were designed to send signals to satellites orbiting in space. The satellite kept track of the birds and beamed the information down to a computer back on earth. Because the small radio was powered by sunlight and not by battery, it was able to operate and follow an osprey for up to three years.

For the first time, scientists could follow ospreys' movements and learn the direction of their routes, whether they take the same route each year, where they stop to feed and rest, the number of days they take to cross land and sea, the approximate number of miles they fly daily, when they arrive in South America and when they depart to return to their breeding grounds. Data on when and where a bird died was now available, too, because their transmitter would stop sending signals. This knowledge would enable people who study raptors to find ways to further protect the species and the places where they live.

Until now, the only way of tracking birds was to capture them and put a metal band around their leg, or to band a young bird still in the nest. The band identified the bird, its location, and date of its banding. This method, however, was highly ineffective because the bird generally had to die for the band to be retrieved, and band returns were rare. Besides, banding offered scant information about a bird's habits and travels.

You may be wondering how KC got his name. KC was the letter code assigned to him when he became a subject for the Highway to the Tropics project. Scientists Dr. Mark Martell, who was in charge of the program, and Dr. Rob Bierregaard, a biology professor at the University of North Carolina, collaborated with Gus Ben David to fit Vineyard ospreys with radio transmitters. KC, his replacement mate, KB, and their neighbors, HX and KD would be followed by the Raptor Center.

Imagine the skill and ingenuity it takes to capture and attach a radio transmitter to an enormous wild bird! Chameli, a golden eagle who belongs to Gus, assisted in the clever plan.

# THE OLD WARRIOR

First, a ten-foot high net, called a mist net, was erected near KC's nest pole. Because an eagle is an osprey's mortal enemy, Gus positioned Chameli close to the net. KC instantly flew down to repel the dangerous intruder. When he did, he became trapped in the net. KC was hooded to calm him, then banded with tags and fitted with a radio backpack. KB, HX, and KD were captured and fitted in the same way. Then they were released to the safety of their nests.

This would be HX's second year in the program. The year before, in June of 2000, HX and his mate, HW, were the first ospreys on Martha's Vineyard—in fact in all of Massachusetts—to be tagged, outfitted, and tracked. This process costs $10,000 per bird, an expense that limits the number of participants.

The pair was followed as they migrated south. The male, HX, made it to Venezuela, traveling about 3,400 miles in 34 days. HW, the female, died in Central America.

Fortunately, HX returned to his nest site in the spring.

It's September 2001. The two couples, KC and KB, and HX and his new mate, KD, are on their way. Only one of them would survive!

The males, KC and HX, followed the

typical migration route south down the east coast, through Florida, Cuba, and Hispaniola, which is an island divided between Haiti and the Dominican Republic, then on to Venezuela. HX returned to exactly the same area where he wintered the year before. Both males arrived by mid-October. The females met with disaster.

KB was lost at sea after landing on a boat as she tried to cross the Caribbean.

KD suffered a similar fate. She also landed on a boat where she apparently died. It's likely that her transmitter was stolen by a crew member because the radio signals continued for a short time back in Haiti and then fell silent.

HX's luck ran out too. HX died in Venezuela. His transmitter stopped signaling in January.

KC made it back! He was like an old

warrior, that bird—tough and experienced. Once again, KC took up his position on the nesting pole he had occupied for over twelve years.

Osprey family life got busy across the Island. Think of what they have to accomplish in this short breeding cycle: establish territory, find a mate, maybe build a nest, lay eggs, incubate, hatch, raise, and fledge their young.

KC failed to produce chicks, so time passed uneventfully for him. In September 2002, he headed south again, carrying with him the silent wishes of his admirers for a safe migration.

# A FIERCE ATTACK

KC's adventures were of such interest now, that newspaper articles were written about him. His fan club grew, and folks looked forward to his spring appearance at the 9th annual Felix Neck Wildlife Sanctuary Osprey Festival.

Families, friends, and neighbors gathered with staff members and volunteers to celebrate the return of the osprey. It was a perfect day. There was not a cloud in the sky, and the sea looked blue as a robin's egg. Amid laughter and games, and plates piled high with homemade treats, Gus strolled, like a roving minstrel, imparting wonders of osprey migration to young and old.

As though on cue, three red-tailed hawks made circles in the sky—a performance that seemed to heighten the audience's anticipation of the main attraction.

But KC didn't show. Gus wasn't worried, though. Not yet.

KC had a habit of showing up late. Last year he missed the festival too. Gus reassured folks pointing out that KC's radio signals were picked up in Cuba. His arrival would be any day now. Still, KC was getting old. He was fifteen or sixteen by now, and that was a concern. Would he have the stamina to continue?

Weeks passed. Gus and his staff waited

anxiously. Slowly, KC made progress. Virginia. Connecticut. On a late April morning, he appeared. But his delay would prove fatal.

A young male challenger sat perched with a female on KC's nest. A nest takeover like this happens occasionally. Often the potential usurper is driven away. KC swooped down to defend his nest site, reenacting a battle as old as time. This struggle was for territory where the strongest would survive.

The younger male met him in the air, and with talons extended, forced KC to the ground. The old warrior recovered and lifted up, but the younger bird continued a fierce attack, intent on expelling KC. KC fought back, but his rival had the advantage of youth and strength. And KC was worn out from his long journey.

KC didn't give up until his opponent inflicted a bad injury that ended the struggle. Triumphant, the younger male drove KC away and claimed his nest.

Defeated and driven from his home,

KC's fate was uncertain now. The wounds he suffered could be serious. If he recovered, would he find somewhere else to settle? He remained in the area and was spotted, once or twice, wandering in the woods.

KC was found dead soon after that.

His transmitter was removed and returned to Felix Neck.

*Perhaps Gus would say that KC's end wasn't sad. Not sad in the world of nature, at any rate, because nature is blind to the existence of all living things. The cycle of birth, struggle, survival, and death goes on according to natural laws. KC's life served one such law: the continuation of the species. KC had fathered many offspring, transmitting his strong genes to succeeding generations. His purpose in nature was over.*

*People, on the other hand, have the ability to think and to feel sad; therefore, they have the capacity to care about wildlife and to make the effort, as Gus Ben David, Mark Martel, Rob Bierregaard, and countless others have, to safeguard the environment and to take steps that contribute to the preservation of creatures that share our magnificent planet.*

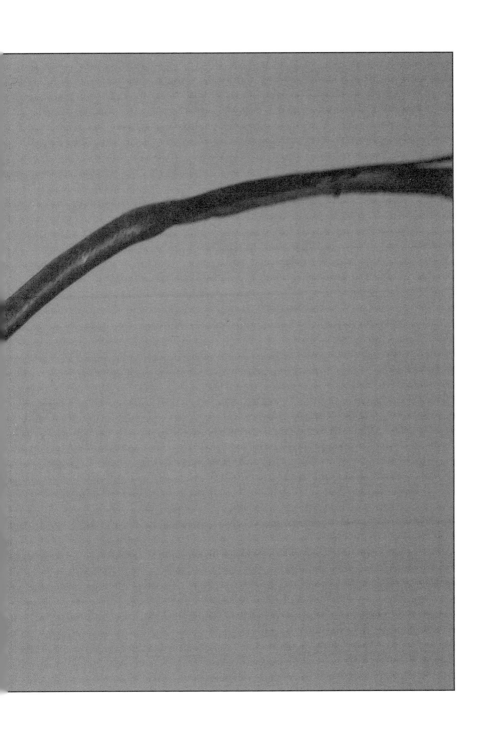

# Glossary

**Breed**
To produce offspring.

**Extinction**
No longer existing.

**Fish Hawk**
Another name for osprey.

**Fledgling**
A young bird that has recently acquired its flight feathers.

**Gene**
That which determines a hereditary characteristic in an organism.

**Habitat**
The area or environment in which an organism lives.

**Incubate**
To warm eggs with the body to promote hatching.

**Instinct**
Natural pattern of behavior; not learned.

**Migration**
Moving from one region or country to another.

**Organism**
An individual form of life, such as a plant or animal.

**Osprey**
A large fish-eating hawk.

**Pesticide**
A chemical used to kill insects.

**Plankton**
Small plant or animal organisms that float in bodies of water.

**Plumage**
The feathers of a bird.

**Predator**
Something that lives by preying on other organisms.

**Raptor**
A bird of prey.

**Rodent**
Mammal with large teeth (incisors) for nibbling or gnawing.

**Satellite**
An object launched to orbit in space.

**Spicules**
Small needle-like spikes on an opsrey's feet.

**Talon**
The long, curved claw of a bird of prey.

**Transmitter**
A device that sends signals.

# Bibliography

## Books

Arnold, Caroline. *Hawk Highway in the Sky: Watching Raptor Migration.* San Diego: Harcourt Brace & Company, 1997.

Dunne, Pete. *The Wind Masters: The Lives of North American Birds of Prey.* Boston: Houghton Mifflin Company, 1995.

Dunne, Pete, David Sibley, and Clay Sutton. *Hawks in Flight: The Flight Identification of North American Migrant Raptors.* Boston: Houghton Mifflin Company, 1988.

Gessner, David. *Return of the Osprey: A Season of Flight and Wonder.* Chapel Hill: Algonquin Books, 2001.

Poole, Alan F. *Ospreys: A Natural and Unnatural History.* Cambridge, UK: Cambridge UP, 1989.

## Articles

Pelikan, Matthew. "Fish Hawk's Migrations Focus of Study; Felix Neck's KC Points Way for Scientists." *The Martha's Vineyard Times,* 9 January 2003: 3, 14.

Robinson, Julian K. "Tracking the Osprey: A Labor of Love." *The Martha's Vineyard Times,* 28 June 2001: sec. Calendar: 22.

Robinson, Julian K. "Drama for Birds, Fun for Kids at Osprey Festival." *The Martha's Vineyard Times,* 11 April 2002: sec: Calendar: 16.

Robinson, Julian K. "Guest of Honor a 'No Show' at Felix Neck." *The Martha's Vineyard Times,* 10 April 2003: sec: Calendar: 9.

Robinson, Julian K. "Osprey Regime Change at Felix Neck." *The Martha's Vineyard Times,* 1 May 2003: sec: Calendar: 17.

Robinson, Julian K. "Sad Postscript to Felix Neck

Osprey Saga." *The Martha's Vineyard Times,* 5 June 2003: sec: Calendar: 23.

## Interviews

Ben David, Augustus. Personal interview. 18 Sept. 2003.

Robinson, Julian K. Personal interview. 19 Sept. 2003.

## Websites

Bierregaard, Rob. "Project Osprey Watch." Rob Bierregaard's Home Page. Department of Biology, University of North Carolina. < http://www.bioweb.uncc.edu/ bierregaard/>

"Ospreys." "Highway to the Tropics." "Migration Tracking." Raptors Via Satellite.": The Raptor Center Home Page. University of Minnesota College of Veterinary Medicine. < http://www.raptor.cvm.umn.edu/>

To find out more about raptors such as eagles, other species of hawks, falcons, vultures, and owls, go to the internet website of the Raptor Center, University of Minnesota College of Veterinary Medicine at: www.raptor.cvm.umn.edu